Poems from my Heart

Marjorie K. Greek

ISBN 979-8-863-00653-6

Printed in the U.S.A.

*I humbly dedicate this book to God,
who has given me the gift of rhyme!*

Foreward

For many years, I wrote poems and stored them in a closet. After a while, I began thinking I should share them, for they might bless or encourage someone who reads them. Now they are published in this book and my earnest desire is that God will be honored in some way as they are read.

I'd like to especially thank my loving husband, David, for his constant support and hours of typing and organizing these poems on the computer. My dear nephew, Greg Alexander, has also been a wonderful support, spending countless hours editing, organizing, and doing all the necessary things to get this book in print. Thank you, Greg! In addition, our two daughters took the time to do a final proofreading of all these poems. Thank you, Kathy and Laura!

Table of Contents

Action

God's Word tells us to praise,
So let our voices raise
And do it!

God's Word says thanks we should give
As long as we live —
So let's do it!

God's Word says we should love
Like the Father above,
So let's do it!

All of these things
And many more
Have been written
By the One we adore
So let's obey;
Yes, obey today!

For He is worthy
And we are not.
He saved us and
Salvation we got.
Thank You, dear Lord!
We will praise You forever!

Amazing Sacrifice!

Lord, as I sit here this morning
And think about You,
I am once again in so much awe
As I contemplate all You went through!

You came down to Earth, had a humble birth;
You gave of Yourself in so many ways —
Then You were willing to be crucified
And ended Your earthly days.

You were despised and forsaken;
You knew sorrow and grief —
Yet when led like a lamb to its slaughter
You were silent as a falling leaf!

You taught us humility, compassion, and love;
You were perfect in every way,
You influenced our world so mightily
That we see the effects every day!

Lord Jesus, how can I ever thank You enough?
You did these things for all humanity
Help me to live as You want me to,
And bring You glory so all can see.

Another One!

Tomorrow when we wake up
It will be a special day!
Yes, it'll be our 68th wedding anniversary
And "Thank You, God" is what we'll say!

Six decades plus eight years together we've had
And our memories are very many.
God blessed us so abundantly
And we could tell stories a-plenty!

Our family that began with the two of us
Has grown to fifty-four!
And before this month is over
A wedding will bring in one more.

Now as we celebrate all this joy,
We are very humbled to think
That in spite of our many imperfect ways
God has filled our cups to the brink!

So on we go, one day at a time,
Enjoying our blessings each day.
And we'll keep on showing our love to each other
As we meet whatever comes our way.

Aware or "Just There"?

God in His abundant love and mercy
Has bestowed on us blessings galore —
But if we don't pay attention
We'll miss much He has in store!

Blessings can easily be overlooked
Unless we are on the alert,
For negative things can crowd right in
And leave us feeling hurt!

So we need to be very aware
And also be ready to receive
All the blessings God has for us —
More than we'd ever believe!

If the whole truth were known,
I believe that each day
We are given a myriad of blessings
Coming to enhance our way!

God made us with two eyes and two ears
So He wants us to be aware —
By looking and listening for His blessings galore
So we'll know for sure that He cares!

When we look for blessings and stay alert,
Our mood will be high, not low!
We'll find those gifts waiting for discovery
And can praise God for the love that He shows!

Best Friend

You're the closest friend I have,
You are always by my side.
I can never feel lonely
For with me You do abide.

Help me, Lord, to trust You daily,
And remember that You care —
All I need to do is come
And speak to You in simple prayer.

You have helped me through my trials,
You have been there when I cried;
I will always praise You, Jesus,
For with me You do abide.

Thank You, Jesus, for Your friendship,
You are always just the same;
You're the One I can depend on,
You are strength for my weak frame!

Blessings

"Thank You" seems so inadequate
As I think of all I've been given!
For You, Lord, have showered me lavishly
All these years that I've been living.

I was born into a loving home
And nurtured with much care —
I was taken to church and learned about You
And found much happiness there.

Many mentors surrounded me
As I grew, observing each one,
They taught me so much about Your love
And how You like things to be done.

I was given excellent teachers
Who taught me to read words on pages —
Then I found lots of excellent books to read
By Christians down through the ages.

You gave me a biological sister,
Plus another from across the sea,
Then brought into my life many more friends
Who were just like sisters to me!

I've enjoyed many, many good times
During all my 79 years,
And in spite of some setbacks and troubles
Why should I have any fears?

Cars

Their job is to get you from here to there,
You can see them around most anywhere!
Yes, the subject is automobiles,
Better known as cars —
Those four wheeled things you
Won't find on Mars!

Some are plush and cost a lot,
But there are also those
That have started to rot!
Some are well-kept and shine like new,
Others are so dirty
You don't want them in view!

Some are strong and can really pull,
Then there are those that hardly go!
They all have horns and steering wheels —
Some are quiet, others have squeals.

Some people's driving we don't like a bit,
So we need to be careful so we don't get hit!
Cars can be a pain, but then of course
Who would want to go back to
Riding a horse?

Christmas Thoughts

God came down in human form
And brought much joy that Christmas morn!
He showed us humility by birth in a manger,
Then He endured many hardships and danger.

But through it all, Jesus did what He heard —
He obeyed the Father and preached His Word!
He gave His life for you and me
As He hung on that cross for all to see!

So now each year we celebrate His birth
Remembering Christ Jesus and His mighty worth.
We give You thanks, dear Lord, for Your Son
And marvel that His sacrifice was for everyone!

Creation

You spoke, God, and the world began —
Each thing came into being.
And now, during my time on Earth,
These miracles of nature I keep seeing.

Day by day, I'm aware of things You've made
And I'm in awe as my spirit lifts;
The trees, the flowers, the shrubs, the grass
Shout silently of Your wonderful gifts.

You've placed me here among Your beauty
And given me eyes and ears.
I've been blessed beyond all measure
Each of my 75 years!

Thank You, Lord, oh thank You;
My heart is full of praise!
May I never take You for granted,
And stay close to You all my days.

Daniel 6 in Verse

There was once a man named Daniel
Who was happy and did what he should —
He loved God and prayed to Him
As often as he could.

Daniel was also very wise
And the King wanted him to rule,
But the other wise men were jealous of him
So they thought of a plan that was cruel.

They told the king to make a new law
Saying all should pray to him,
And then if they refused to pray to the king
They'd be thrown in the lion's den.

Now Daniel knew all about the law
But he prayed to God, not the king!
For he loved God so very much
He wasn't afraid of anything!

The bad wise men were peeking,
And they caught Daniel saying his prayers.
So they took him to the king and tattled,
"We saw Daniel pray to God over there!"

"Let's throw him in the lion's den,"
All those jealous men cried.
The king felt bad since he liked Daniel,
But he couldn't change the law if he tried

So into the den of lions went Daniel
And he had to stay all night!
Early the next day the king hurried over
To see if Daniel was all right.

"I'm fine," said Daniel, "because an angel came
And closed the mouth of each lion.
I never have to worry about God
For He protects me all the time!"

So remember, you don't have to worry either —
Just say a little prayer;
Ask God to help you in your troubles
And you can be sure He'll be there!

David and Goliath

David was a nice young boy
Who took care of sheep for his dad.
His older brothers were away in Saul's army
And they needed some food very bad.

So David's dad told him to go
And take his brothers some bread;
When he got there he saw Goliath
Who was a giant with a big body and head.

Now Saul's whole army was made up of God's people
And Goliath served with the other guys —
He wanted one of Saul's soldiers to fight him
But everyone was afraid of his size.

When David heard this and saw the giant
He stepped right up and said, "Let me."
But Saul said, "You are only a boy,
Goliath is bigger than you, can't you see?"

"Yes," answered David, "but God will help me,
Because I know He's my friend and my Lord."
So Saul said "Okay," took off his armor
And gave David his helmet and sword.

But when David put on all those heavy things
He did not want them at all —
"I'd rather use my little sling and some stones,
For with those I can make him fall."

Goliath stepped closer to David, the boy,
So David put a stone in his sling,
Then quick as a wink, he twirled the band
And gave that stone a fling!

Well, guess what? The stone hit Goliath's forehead
And that big giant fell down!
David was glad that he'd trusted God,
And all of God's people gathered happily around.

Easter Time Thoughts

Lord, how You did it, I'll never know;
It's all a mystery to me.
You gave up all You had in heaven
When You came down to Calvary.

I read Your story with wonder and awe;
How could that much love be in You?
And yet I know that it's a fact
For each Word in Your Book is true.

You walked our Earth with humility and truth,
Compassion and love marked Your path.
Yet in loneliness Your life ended here,
As You received the public's wrath.

You willingly hung on that old rugged cross
While wearing Your crown of thorns —
Then amazingly You called out to God
To forgive those who showed only scorn!

My heart aches for You, my Lord
When I think of Your suffering and shame.
And I am humbled when I think of myself,
How little things make me complain.

Thank You, Lord, for Your sacrifice
That was full of such wonderful love,
And help me never to forget all You did
When You came for my sake from above!

Enough

Peace of mind is a wonderful gift
And this is what God has given –
He sent His Son Jesus to die on the cross
So believers can all go to Heaven!

There are many in the world today
Who think they must prove they are good,
So they fill their lives with lots of works
And wear out more than they should!

But God's Word tells us plainly
We're saved by faith alone,
So we don't have to strive, strive, and strive
And slave ourselves to the bone!

However, faith without works is dead
So we do things to show God our love.
We aren't working our way to heaven at all —
We just want to honor God above!

Evening Quiet Time

The night is quiet, the hour is late,
Most folks I know are fast asleep!
But this is a special hour for me
As I come to the Lord my quiet time to keep.

You are always there, Lord, waiting for me.
I know You want my fellowship regularly each day,
And so I want to please You and get to know You better.
Please help me be consistent — I know there is a way!

Your Word is here and free to all,
We just need to take the time
To meet You privately in quiet,
Then our spirits will be sublime.

And when we leave You to do our work
We'll be refreshed and strong
To deal with all the challenges in life,
And in our hearts will always be a song!

Friends

Friends are special gifts in life,
They come in a variety of ways.
You can meet them almost anywhere
On any kind of days!

They themselves are a mixed variety,
Tall, short, large and small.
They can be your age, older or younger,
But it doesn't matter at all!

For when you find a kindred spirit
You both know it very soon —
You'll feel so comfortable with that one
That your heart will hum a tune!

This happy gift of good friends
Can come when you least expect it,
And he or she will brighten your life
So you will not regret it!

Now here is a special bit of news —
We can have a friend better than any other!
His name is Jesus Christ the Lord!
He loves us even more than a brother!

For what friend do you know that would give their life
Just because they loved you very much?
Jesus did that very thing —
When He died on the cross for us!

Friendship

Friendship is a happy word
That is closely related to love;
Both of these are gifts to us
That come from our Father above.

Sometimes we find it with one special person,
Then other times, we're in groups where it blooms!
But no matter how many or few there are,
Friends bring us joy, not gloom!

Since friendship is all about relationships,
These can often start with us;
It could be a smile you give at church
Or a listening ear to someone on a bus!

Some important things we need to remember
As we grow in our friendship with others —
Is to be humble and forgiving, and keep in mind
That we, too, sin like our sisters and brothers!

So let's enjoy this wonderful gift
And thank God for being so kind —
Be on the alert as you go your way
For many new friends you may find!

God Be Glorified

God, You are my Maker
And I love You so much!
I pray to You this morning
That I can feel Your tender touch.

I want to give You all the glory,
Honor, love and praise,
So when I go about my tasks,
Help me my thoughts to raise.

And when I do a deed or two
That helps someone today,
Please let Your Spirit remind me
That I am but the clay.

You are the Master Molder
Who has made a vessel of me;
Teach me to give You the credit
So all around can see.

I don't want the glory,
It all belongs to You —
Lord, glorify Yourself today
In everything I do.

God In Nature

You have made it all, Lord
With Your infinite wisdom and skill.
Your loving generosity is there to see,
We can observe it if we will.

You've made so much variety, Lord —
No two things are the same.
We cannot possibly comprehend all this
So we'll just say, "Praise Your Name!"

Your mercies are new every morning
For Your compassions never end.
We know You are in sovereign control
And You're our best true Friend.

Thank You, Father, for this world
In which we spend our days,
And help us as we live our lives
To bring to You our praise!

God's Comfort

Thank You, Lord, for comfort,
For being there for me.
I know that You have promised
That I can lean on Thee.

And when I see a friend
Who has just become bereaved,
I also see the ways in which
You help her as she grieves.

You work in many awesome ways,
Your wonders to perform,
And special blessings that I see
Just become the norm!

I love You, Lord, and thank You
For Your steady constant love;
I know that I can count on You
To send comfort from above.

I also know Your Spirit indwells
And is a loyal Friend.
He's there to help and lean on
As my emotions begin to mend.

So thank You, God, for caring,
And lending me Your aid.
For as I meet life's trials with You
I never need be afraid!

His Fragrance in My Life

Lord, I'm aware of Your fragrance each day,
I have only to look out and see
The wonderful variety around my home
And I know You've caused it all to be!

I enjoy the colors, sizes, and shapes
As I see trees, and flowers around,
Or listen to the songs of birds in the trees —
All these cause my joy to abound!

Then, Lord, as I read Your wonderful Word,
I'm aware of Your fragrance so sweet,
For Your Book of love is filled with Your grace
And it makes me want to bow at Your feet!

You reveal Yourself to me all the time
In my family and friends through the days;
Lord, I could fill many, many a book
With praise to You for Your ways!

There is music to be played and listened to,
There are wonderful books to read,
There are people to see and pets to love —
Lord, You meet my every need!

And now, Lord, I'm thinking of what I can do
To let others see Your fragrance in me —
I think that one of the best things to do
Is let the fruits of Your Spirit flow free

There's only one way I know this can happen
And that is to constantly walk
Close to You, Lord, each moment I live
So my life will be more than just talk.

You've shown me Your fragrance in so many ways,
Now please help me to spread it for You;
Lord, You are my daily source of beauty,
Let it shine in all that I do.

If Lael Could Talk

It was dark and wet, warm and comfy
When I began to grow last November.
I heard my mommy and daddy's voices
And that's about all I remember!

The months flew by and I grew and grew;
I loved riding around in Mama's bod!
I didn't know much as the days went by,
But Someone knew everything and it was God!

He knew what they would find
When they ran a special test —
I had some missing parts
But still God knew best!

I stayed inside my mommy
Until it was the right time.
And then I was born,
But things weren't all fine.

I needed some kidneys to live on Earth
And I never got any at all —
So after I had stayed 30 minutes,
I went to Heaven to answer God's call.

Those 30 minutes on Earth were very sweet —
My parents tenderly and lovingly held me.
I felt your warmth and deep love
And I was happy and contented as could be!

But God has His perfect plan
That we don't always understand.
He sent me to Heaven where there is no harm
And I am now perfect in Jesus' arms!

And though you have to wait awhile
To hold me again and give me love,
Please know that all is well with me
'Cause I'm with God and Jesus above!

This poem was written soon after Lael, our 20th great-grandchild, left this Earth to be with Jesus. The hope was to help her parents and all of us who were grieving her loss. This intent, I believe was realized. Thanks be to You, Lord!

Independence Day

Every year on the very same date
We Americans celebrate our land.
There are parades, picnics and fireworks
And many places have a band.

In churches throughout the nation
Folks lift their voices in praise,
For we are all so grateful
That God has blessed our days.

But little by little, through the years,
Sin has crept into our land,
Until now the values our founders proclaimed
Have been distorted on every hand.

The problem lies in people's hearts —
They have moved away from the Lord.
The prosperity and blessing we've all been given
Are taken for granted, while God's ignored.

It must grieve the Lord to see this sin
And watch men stray from Him;
We need a repentance and revival here,
A turning from our sin.

Time is running out for the U.S.A.,
God's patience will end one day!
Each heart needs to examine itself —
We need to turn to the Lord and pray

John 3:16 in Verse

First there was God, who is love,
He gave us His Son from above!
Jesus left all His comforts to come to Earth
And if we receive Him, we'll have a new birth.

His spirit will indwell us every day of our life
And we will have guidance, comfort and peace during strife.
There is no better way to face each new day
Than to walk with our Lord and humbly obey.

God gave the supreme gift and He patiently waits
Until we invite Him in —
Then there is peace that can never depart,
For His spirit lives forever within our heart.

Laughter

Laughter is a wonderful gift from God,
After you do it, you feel good in your bod!
Unleashes some tensions and brightens your day,
Gladdens your heart in a wonderful way!
Hee haws are fun, especially with friends;
Thanks to God for the good vibes they send!
Easy to do, they don't cost a cent!
Render us happiness so we're content!

Lavish Love

Lord, Your lavish love pours out to me
Each day that I'm on Earth.
You have always shown how much You care,
Constantly since the day of my birth.

When I open my eyes every morning
And see all the things You have made,
When I listen to the songs of the birds and the wind
I recognize these gifts that You gave!

The sunrises and sunsets, the glory of the skies
Continue to give me a show —
Your love is around me day and night,
Just everywhere that I go!

And, Lord, the friends that You have put in my life
I know are a gift from You;
They bless me richly in so many ways,
They show Your love in what they do.

Lord, I could write on and on about all You do,
As You shower me with love every day.
But there's no way I could thank You enough
For all Your lavish gifts along the way.

So, Lord, please accept my gratitude
For Your love, so lavish and free —
I will keep on living to honor You
So others will see You in me

Life

Life is a gift that comes from God,
It's a mystery in many ways.
How can a seed that is buried in dirt
Change to a growing plant in days?

And how can the tiniest egg unite
With an equally tiny cell,
Then grow into an amazing babe
That can breathe, move, and think so well?

Only God knows these answers
So we need to trust in Him always
And thank Him each day for the life He gives
As we travel this Earth, all our days.

So, what is life? Jesus said He was Life;
He also said he's the Way and the Truth!
Since He said this, we believe it for sure —
Then we'll have life after we leave this Earth.

Jesus said, "I am the Way, the Truth and the Life
And he who believes in Me will never perish."
So let's all follow Him, so we'll meet in heaven
And continue this life that we cherish!

Lights for Jesus

You, Lord, left heaven and came to us —
A light, to show the way.
Now it's our turn to shine as we live
And go about our lives each day.

We absorb our radiance from You alone
By spending time with You.
Then as we spend our time with others,
Your light comes shining through!

It's not a secret; there's no magic —
It's very simple and clear!
It just takes practice and focus on You
So that we're aware You are near!

We need to remember Your Spirit indwells us
And is a constant reliable source.
When we need some help along the way
We can count on You to guide our course.

And as we learn to rely on Your power,
Your light through us shines brighter;
Then the lives that You bring for us to touch
Find their burdens seem a little lighter!

So help us, Lord, to remember our part
As on our earthly paths we go —
Let's stay connected to our wonderful Source
So we can glow and glow!

Love
(Based on I Corinthians 13)

Love is a simple four-letter word
That is very easy to spell;
Yet to actually show it and feel it inside
Is something that's hard to do well.

God tells us that love is essential —
Greater than faith and hope,
And it needs to be deep in our hearts
As with our lives we cope.

Even if we gave all to the poor,
Or our martyred bodies were burned,
Without love there would be no meaning,
And no spiritual reward would be earned.

We are told that love is patient,
It's also kind and true,
It never fails, gives hope in all things,
And endures in all we do.

We have God's wonderful example
Of sending His only Son —
This was the ultimate sacrifice,
To show His love for everyone.

Yet here on Earth we have trouble,
Being loving for even a day;
We are busy caring for our own needs,

Could it be that the reason we're weak,
And have trouble with real love
Is because we don't spend enough time,
Getting to know our Father above?

Maturity comes with study and prayer,
And God's love can be more than just talk,
We can be filled with His love each day of our life,
And reflect Him to all in our walk.

Mary, Mother of Jesus
(Based on Luke 1)

Her name was Mary, she was just a girl,
But for her, God had a job like no other.
He wanted her to be the one
That would be the Lord Jesus Christ's mother!

Now Mary did not know this plan at all
When with Joseph she fell in love,
But soon God sent a special angel
Who came from heaven above.

The angel spoke to her and said,
"Mary, the Lord is with you!"
Poor Mary did not understand this a bit
And she didn't know what to do.

"Don't fear," said the angel, "for you have pleased God,
You'll have a babe God will send —
His name will be Jesus; He will be great
And His Kingdom will have no end."

"But how can this be?" asked sweet young Mary,
"For I am not yet wed."
"God's Spirit and power will come upon you,"
The helpful angel said.

So Mary was pregnant with Jesus
And soon gave birth to her Son.
He was born in a lowly stable

Now that is the story of Mary,
Who God used in a wonderful way.
He has a plan for each one of us
If we love Him and try to obey.

It doesn't matter how old you are
Or if you are rich or poor!
It just matters if you want to please Him —
Then He will use you for sure!

Missions

Lord, You've given us our life
And You've put us on this Earth.
You sent Your Son to save us —
Belief in Him gives new birth.

We are each in a special location;
There are people near that we know —
You've told us You want the gospel spread
And You want each believer to go.

It may not be far away from home
That You desire Your servant's work,
So help us to ever be aware
And not be willing to shirk.

Help us, Lord, to be free from fear,
Help us spread the gospel for You.
Let us concentrate on this and not our rejection
And then we can reach out and do!

Why are we here? And what is God's will?
The answers are always the same —
We are to bring glory to You,
To plant seeds that will bring praise to Your name.

Jesus came and Jesus died,
God was man for awhile.
Oh, the wonderful gift of grace —
It always makes my heart smile!

Morning Quiet Time

Good morning, Lord! I'm here again
To spend some time with You.
I've had a night of restfulness
So this is the next thing I'll do.

My heart is full of gratitude
As I think of all You've done —
You've created me and loved me, too,
And You've done this for everyone!

The world of nature boggles my mind
As I see its vast array.
Your generosity, variety, and orderliness
Are displayed for me each day!

I'm grateful, too, for all my senses:
Sight, hearing, touch, taste, and smell.
For without this gift, I could not fully enjoy
This world You have made so well.

The people You've brought into my life
Have enriched me in many ways.
Each one has brought something unique —
For this I give You praise!

Moses

He was just a tiny baby,
So innocent and sweet,
But he had to be hidden from the king
So his mother was very discreet.

She made a special basket
And tucked him in just right,
Then hid it in the river
Where he was out of sight.

And then his sister Miriam
Went down to stay near him,
For she knew that if he fell out
He wouldn't know how to swim!

Well, pretty soon a girl came by —
She was the king's own daughter!
She wanted to take a bath that day
So went down to the river's water.

She was very surprised to see
The basket with a baby in it.
She thought he was so precious
And loved him from the first minute!

In fact, she loved him so much
She decided to take him home,
And there she planned to raise him
And treat him like her own!

Now Miriam hurried to the princess
And asked if she'd like help with her brother;
The princess said "yes" so Miriam ran
And got her very own mother!

Then the three of them went to the palace —
The princess and the babe, his mom, too!
That's how God took care of Moses
And He'll also take care of you!

Motherhood

What can compare with the joy of giving birth?
This tiny new life has been born from me!
And so starts a whole new aspect of living
That will continue far into the future — you'll see!

The baby God gave you is fragile and small —
She depends on you for every care.
Day after day the mothering continues,
And you are so glad that you can be there.

The little one grows and gains independence;
Yet your ongoing nurturing still needs to be.
It's a hard, busy time of physical work,
But the joy of the mothering flows freely.

Many prayers are needed as the days go by,
For there is much the child must learn;
And not only the child, but the mom as well —
Oh, the myriad of things she must discern!

The days fly by, there is so much to do!
Laundry, meals, and duties abound,
Yet the underlying joy remains untouched
For motherhood is a sacred calling, I've found!

Then one day your heartstrings are pulled
As your little ones, matured, start leaving the nest,
And you say your prayers that they have learned
All the lessons they need to make choices that are best!

That's when your walk with God grows deeper,
And you learn to go with the flow.
For you know you've done all that you could —
Now you must give your child to God as you let him/her go.

You also start realizing
That prayer for your child, now grown,
Is so very powerful and necessary
To nurture the seeds you have sown.

The One who has been with you constantly
Is still the same — and near,
So there's no need to spend time worrying
And He doesn't want you to fear.

Your job of raising your child
Will eventually come to an end
And then you will reap the rewards of mothering
As you realize your child is now your good friend!

My Aging Adventure #1

I had a birthday not long ago
And it made me 77!
Now this is very hard to believe
Since inside I feel only 20 plus ! !

It's true my body is slowing down
And it's hard to jump rope or run,
But those limitations haven't spoiled my life
And I still have lots and lots of fun!

For deep inside me I know who I am —
A blessed daughter of the King!
And no matter how old I live to be,
That's the most important thing!

I love the Lord with all my heart
And my gratitude continues to grow
As I realize He is letting me stay here on Earth
Where I can serve Him anywhere I go.

For He's told us to let our light so shine
That others may see our works that are good.
Then they will glorify His holy name
And give honor to Him, as they should.

So I keep on aging and learning more
About how I must live for my Lord,
And I'm really enjoying this new adventure
For I never, never get bored!

Thank You God, for loving me,
For letting me live all these years —
And when You decide You want me in heaven
I'll leave here without any fears!

My Aging Adventure #2

My aging adventure has continued
And seven more years are gone —
I'm now an 84-year-old lady
But I still can sing a song!

Yes, I'm getting closer to heaven,
But I feel as young as can be;
I may look old and wrinkly,
But inside is a young happy me!

For I know I have a Savior
And His spirit dwells within;
This knowledge gives me lots of joy,
I know I can depend on Him!

And even though I'm slowing down
There still are ways to serve —
Plus God keeps right on blessing me
With things I don't deserve!

So I'm a "happy camper"
And am grateful each new day;
It's still a great adventure!
I enjoy my earthly stay!

My Desire

This day is beginning,
So quiet and still.
I come before You, Lord —
I want to do Your will!

Please continue to guide and protect me —
I want to please You.
Keep me teachable and loving
In all that I do!

I love You and thank You, Lord —
You've been my ultimate friend!
You are my fortress and my hiding place
And on You I can always depend!

My cup of blessings is running over,
I know this is very true!
Help me to be a shining light today
In everything I do!

My Gratitude

Lord, You are so good to me!
You give me life each day!
You let me have good eyes and ears,
You listen when I pray.

You've given me a sweet little pup
And a husband for 50 years!
You reveal Yourself in so many ways,
In my laughter as well as my tears.

How can I possibly thank You enough
For Jesus who died for me?
I have no fear about leaving this Earth
For I know just where I'll be!

I'll be spending eternity in heaven with You,
Where there's no more sorrow or pain.
I'll be able to praise and exalt You there
For that's where You forever will reign.

So, thank You, thank You, thank You, Lord God,
To You I give all my praise!
I'll exalt You with my lips and heart
As I live out the rest of my days.

My Quiet Time

I woke up early this morning,
I couldn't go back to sleep.
And so I came to my little room,
My time with You, Lord, to keep.

I need this quiet time each morn
To read Your Word and pray.
It helps my thoughts stay directed toward You
Each hour of my day.

It's more than a foolish compulsion,
It's not a passing whim.
It's a precious time of fellowship,
As I share that hour with Him.

I love You, Lord, I adore You —
I want to meet every day.
I need my special time with You,
It makes me feel good in all ways.

So thank You for being there for me,
For waiting with open arms;
I know You'll never let me down
And You'll shield me from all life's harms.

Noah
(Based on Genesis 6)

God gave Noah a big job to do,
So Noah began right away.
He took his hammer, nails, and wood
And worked hard night and day.

He didn't care that people might laugh
And think he was kind of dumb,
For God had told him to get the Ark made
Before the flood began to come.

Noah built everything the way God ordered
And then he brought the animals by twos;
Soon his family and the creatures, great and small,
Were in the Ark, ready for the cruise!

The rain fell steadily for 40 days and nights,
It kept coming and coming from the sky.
The flood wiped out all the life on Earth
Except for Noah and his crew, who were dry!

Finally the rain stopped and God said to leave,
Then He set a rainbow in the cloud.
This meant He promised no more huge floods —
Rain covering the Earth wouldn't be allowed.

After the flood Noah lived quite awhile;
His sons and their families did, too.
They all were happy that Noah obeyed God
And did what he was told to do.

On Creation

Thank You, Lord, for nature
And all You've made for us;
I look around me every day
And am awed by Your creativeness.

You didn't make a dull array
Of just one shape, size or hue
Instead, I see a myriad of things
And they all remind me of You!

I love You, Lord, and honor Your Name
I praise You for all of these things
I thank You for my senses
And the pleasure Your creation brings.

On Prayer

Prayer is not hard to do at all,
It is simply talking to You.
So, why is it that many times
It's the very last thing I do?

I do not mean to slight You,
I love You very much!
So please forgive my negligence
When I don't keep in touch.

Help me keep You foremost,
In my thoughts each hour,
And then I know I'll walk much straighter,
For You will give me the power.

Thank You for Your Spirit,
Who indwells me all the time;
He's waiting very patiently,
For me to give Him my mind.

Our Challenging, Interesting Adventure

Lord, You are blessing Dave and me so well,
You are letting us together grow old!
The journey has its ups and downs —
Some are surprising as they begin to unfold!

We notice our bodies aren't as able as they were,
And we seem to tire faster than before.
But as we rest and enjoy life together,
We have interesting times reminiscing, more and more!

The myriad of blessings You've heaped on us
Come crowding into my mind.
So daily I'm thanking You for Your love,
And how You have been so kind!

Yet thanks doesn't seem enough to say,
For You've showered me with kindness galore.
So I want to fill my life full of love to You
As I continue to journey some more!

Our Tribute

This is a tribute of gratitude
To God, who has guided our way.
He's the reason we can celebrate
Our golden anniversary today!

He helped us find each other
Even before we had thought to pray!
He's provided for us through all these years,
And He's helped us in every way.

He's given us children and their spouses —
The number is four plus four;
And then He lavished us with His love
By sending sweet grandchildren galore!

We didn't have any idea
Back in June, 1955,
That we would be given all of these years
And today we'd still be alive!

So here we are with grateful hearts
Full of adoration and praise!
We want to bring God glory
As we live out the rest of our days.

Our Trip

We left on our trip
And were gone many days.
We're now going home
With hearts full of praise.

Lot of miles were traveled
By car and by air,
Many people we've visited,
Here and there.

We've see much beauty
In three different states.
We ate lots of food
'Cause we filled up our plates!

We enjoyed visiting
Many relatives and friends,
32 people in all,
And there the list ends.

Now it's on to our next
Blessed chapter of life.
Home again, home again,
Happy husband and wife!

Thank You, Lord!

Overflowing Cup

Today I'm thinking about my "cup" —
My gratitude cup God's given me.
It's actually running over these days.
Why is that you ask? Read this and see!

My 90th birthday came recently
And how blessed that made me feel.
To have these years of longevity
Makes God's love even more real!

Added to that in my cup
Is Dave's 90th birthday, too!
We are grateful to grow old together
As we share in the things we do!

Another big blessing in my cup
Is the wonderful time we had
When family traveled from far and near
To celebrate and make us glad!

A gala party was prepared
With lots of toil and love,
And seeing so many family members
Made me praise my Father above!

Then, coming soon is another baby,
He'll be a sweet little boy —
Number 23 in our group of great-grandkids
And we know he'll fill us with joy!

So you see why my cup overflows
As I'm blessed with all these things.
They keep on coming and coming
And all this makes my heart sing!

Thank You, God!

Paths

There are just two paths to take in life —
One is wrong, the other right.
The wrong one fills you with worry and unrest,
While the right one gives you peace that is best.

There will be problems along either way,
But the right one gives you strength each day,
While the other leaves you fretting
As you wander astray.

Can you guess what these paths are?
One is to believe and follow Christ,
The other is to go your own way,
And stray each day.

If you follow Christ and do His Will,
Your days with peace and joy He'll fill.
And best of all, when life here ends,
You'll be with Jesus and your believing friends!

Psalm 23 in Verse

God, You are my Shepherd; I know this is true.
You watch over me in all that I do.
So why should I worry and fret and despair,
When I know You are faithful and You're always there?

You lead me in places so serene and calm,
You minister to me like a healing balm.
My soul is restored, I can go on living,
For You just keep on giving and giving.

You love me and guide me to walk in right ways
And I know You'll be faithful to bless all my days.
Even when death's dark shadow is near,
I don't have to panic, I don't have to fear!

You comfort and strengthen and hold me tight,
Early in the morning, late at night.
When enemies are present, You help me then, too,
For You are with me in all that I do.

Lord, there is no end to Your goodness and love,
They fit over my life just like a glove.
And when, here on Earth, I no longer will roam,
I know that eternally I'll share Your home!

Poem for a Gloomy Day

The sun is hiding behind the clouds,
The sky is gray and dim,
But I must find a way to feel
Happy and cheerful within.

First I'll eat a cookie
And then hum a little tune;
For you it's probably a cup of coffee
And read the paper til noon!

There, now I feel a wee bit better,
In fact, I can actually smile.
But if I forget and look outside
I'll probably be glum yet awhile.

So maybe I'll go and see a friend,
Or quicker, just make a phone call.
And before I know it, I've forgotten the gloom
And the clouds don't matter at all.

But then the phone call is over,
The house looks dusty and dark.
The beds aren't made, the wash isn't done
And the dogs do nothing but bark!

Now, I've got to face this dingy day
And I don't really want to feel bad,
So I'll try to concentrate on my blessings —
I know there are plenty to be had!

Dear Lord, You've given me another new day,
And I do have this house to live in.
It gives me warmth and privacy
And a place to show love to my kin.

So help me to change my attitudes
And give my blues the run.
After all, if it weren't for these cloudy days
I might not appreciate Your sun!

Praise God!

God, You have done so very much,
I don't know where to start!
You've always been and always will be
And You dwell within my heart!

My birth has come, not once, but twice,
Both were a gift from You.
You've cared for me for 70 years
And You're with me in all I do!

You created the world and everything in it —
You are in charge of land and sea.
You alone have all the power
And yet You care for me!

The glory that all nature displays
Makes me daily rejoice.
You have done such awesome, wonderful things
And yet You hear my voice!

From the tiniest ant to the enormous whale,
Your majesty is revealed.
Then I think how You cared enough for me
And how through Jesus Your love was revealed.

Your humility puts me to utter shame,
You gave up Your only Son —
He went through death on the cross for me.
In fact, He died for everyone!

I read in Your Book You took care of folks
Back in Moses' day.
You led them out of cruel bondage
And guided them all the way.

You were patient with them when they complained,
You gave manna and quail to eat.
And though they wandered for 40 years
Their shoes didn't rot on their feet!

The stories You've told in that Book of Yours
Are all inspiring to me:
Joseph, Abraham, Rahab, Mary —
Their faith is there to see.

So, loving God, I bow to You
And thank You every day
For all Your love and blessings
As I journey along my way!

Psalm 139 in Verse

Everything I do, Lord, is known ahead by You,
So there is nothing I can hide, no matter what I do.
You know my every movement and every word I'll say,
You are aware of thoughts I have even before I pray!

I do not understand all this,
It is too much for me.
I only know that it's a fact
You have this ability.

I marvel at my body
That You so intricately designed;
Even one of my small fingers
Has parts I cannot define!

You created me so quietly
Within my mother's womb.
You've woven me into Your plan,
I was on Your wonderful loom!

You even had all my days in Your Book
Before one of them came to be!
So I need not worry about the length of my life
'Cause You'll call when You're ready for me.

I also know, Lord, You are always here,
Every step of my way.
That is why I can feel Your peace
Every moment of each day.

God, words are not enough for me
To express my wonder and love.
I only know that You are great
And You rule from above.

Really?

Each day brings me 24 hours closer!
The time is drawing near...
Yes, I know it's coming —
My 90th birthday this year!

And yet, I have trouble believing it's true,
Am I really going to be that old?
I've always thought that 90 was ancient,
At least I think that's what I've been told.

I just pinched myself to help me believe
That I've lived all these years and am this old.
But in spite of the telltale changes in my body,
I'm young at heart and grateful as each day unfolds!

For I know God is with me and blesses so much
And He has reasons to keep me here this long.
So I'll live my life to please Him,
As I keep in my heart a song!

Resident or President?

We open our hearts to You, Lord,
As we believe in Jesus, Your Son.
We accept Your gift of eternal life
And we know You're the Holy One.

So we have Your Spirit residing in us
Because of our faith in You,
But are we letting You lead and guide
In everything we think, say, and do?

Do I push my selfishness out of the way
And look for Your guidance for me?
Please help me to live totally under Your rule,
So Your bright light will shine for all to see!

I want You to be the Head of my life,
I'm glad You are now a resident.
But I need to be willing in all I do
To let You also act as President!

Saturated!

Lord, You are a master at filling;
You've poured so much of Yourself into me!
Your love and forgiveness saturate my life
And there's so much more I can see!

I'm overwhelmed by all You've done these years —
Patience and joy and kindness abound.
Your friendship is like no other I have,
And the peace You've given the world has not found.

Yes, my cup is running over —
This is so very true!
Thanks doesn't seem an adequate word
For me to say to You.

So, as I sit here today, full of gratitude,
And think how You've saturated me,
I know what I can give in return for all this —
It's my wholehearted will turned over to Thee.

So, I will try harder to reflect Jesus' light
In all that I think, say, and do.
Then when I graduate to Your heavenly home
Your saturation in my life will shine through!

Spiritual Millionaire

Day after day, Lord, I'm blessed by You —
I can see Your hand in so much that I do!
You are enhancing my life in SO many ways
And I'm grateful to You for all of these days!

Time after time, You have guided and loved —
Sometimes I don't see Your gifts from above!
There are so many I can't count them all,
Yet You keep giving in winter, spring, summer, and fall!

So I want to thank You and give You praise,
For without You, I would be a mess —
You are my rock and my hiding place
And You are the very, very best!

Help me, Lord, to trust You more
And be aware of what I'm still here for.
I want to please You in every way
As I live these last years on Earth each day!

Senses

The heavens declare the glory of God,
Each day we see a new show!
And here on Earth all the beauty of nature
Makes my awe and gratitude grow.

All this beauty You've made for me,
I see it daily in earth and sky.
May I never become complacent
And take for granted my eyes!

The songs of the birds have lifted my spirit,
As I've listened down through the years.
The wind in the trees and the waves on the shore
Make me thank You, Lord, for my ears.

The fragrance of newly mown grass
And the gentle scent of the rose,
The smell of pines in the forest —
These make me glad for my nose!

Daily, I enjoy the food I eat —
There are so many wonderful flavors.
So, I thank You, God, for my sense of taste
That allows me my food to savor.

Last, but not least, is my sense of touch
That enhances the world I live in.
I use it in many ways each day
And am grateful that You have given it.

So, thank You, Lord, for the senses You've given —
Each one is a blessing indeed.
With Your infinite wisdom and lavish love
You've given us all that we need!

Spring

There's expectancy in the air —
All of nature is beginning to awake.
God's creation, once again,
Is shouting praises for His sake!

The buds are getting larger,
The bulbs are opening slowly,
The birds are chirping happily,
And I'm feeling humble and lowly.

For I know the Creator is alive and well
As His glory is silently shown.
Everywhere I look right now
Reminds me that He's on His throne!

Thank You, Father, for spring,
When dormancy comes to an end
And our senses are filled with wonder
As we see the life that You send.

And most of all, let me remember
The source of new life in me —
Your Son, my wonderful Savior,
Whom You sent to die on that tree.

This life that is mine forever
Has no spring, winter, summer, or fall;
It is with me in every season
And it's available for all!

Thank You, Lord!

Sunrise, Sunset, SUNRISE!

It all begins when we are born,
Our sunrise here on Earth!
Just as each day that we are here,
God's sun shines, giving the day its birth!

The days, weeks, months, and years go by
As we live our varied lives;
Soon, it seems, the end is near,
And death severs our earthly ties.

The sunset comes, and people grieve
As the one they love leaves for good —
Yes, sunset will come for all of us
Just as God planned it would!

But wait! This sunset becomes a SUNRISE!
For Jesus paid the price for our sin!
And for those who believe this and accept His gift,
Eternity will be ours with Him!

Thankfulness

We've been told to give God thanks
No matter what we're going through,
For we know He's there to help us
In everything we do.

An attitude of gratefulness
Will give to God the glory
And then when others ask us why
We can tell them our sweet story.

For it isn't so much what we have to endure
But it's how we accept each new thing;
God's Spirit indwells us to make us strong
And He helps to lessen the sting.

We are spiritual millionaires each day we live,
Because God has poured out His love.
So let's try to remember to give Him our thanks
So He will rejoice from above!

Thanksgiving

Thank You, God, for who You are!
Hear our prayers from near and far.
Answers, we know, will come in Your time —
Now or later — we know it'll be fine!
Knowledge of You is what we need,
Salvation You offer — by this we are freed!
Giving, giving is what You do —
In our hearts we know that this is true!
Very blessed each day that we are living,
In every way, You keep giving, giving!
Now we gather to praise and thank You —
Gratitude fills our minds, through and through!

Thanksgiving Celebration

This is the month we celebrate
God's blessings to us the past year.
We gather together with family and friends,
Some come far, some are near.

We sit down to eat our Thanksgiving feast
With hearts full of gratitude,
For we know there are many less fortunate
And we must not have a blasé attitude.

God has blessed us richly
Way beyond what we could have hoped for.
He has given us freedom, wealth, and family
And, oh, so very much more!

So this Thanksgiving as we gather
We will remember God and His love.
And hopefully we won't be thankful just a day
But will constantly send praises above.

The Garden

Daddy planted seeds,
Mommy picked the weeds,
And the kids watched the garden grow.
Each one did his part from the very start
But God did the most, you know!

'Cause He made the seeds and the water, too,
And He made the people great and small —
Without His tender care, no one would be there,
So let us thank Him, one and all.

The First Christmas

It happened one dark night,
Long before the light of day,
Mary gave birth to a baby boy
And laid Him in the hay.

This special boy was God's only Son
And from heaven is where He came.
Mary and Joseph called Him Jesus,
For an angel told Mary to call Him that name.

Outside on the hills where the shepherds were,
An angel appeared in the sky.
Some of the shepherds were so afraid
They probably started to cry!

But the angel said, "Do not be afraid —
I am going to tell you good news.
God's Son has just been born in town,
And you may see Him, if you choose!"

Then lots and lots of angels appeared,
And they all gave God their praises.
The shepherds decided to go see the babe
And they had happy looks on their faces.

After they made the trip to the manger
They left and were full of joy!
They told everyone the wonderful news
About this special little boy.

So that's what happened the very first Christmas,
You can read in your Bible the story.
God sent His Son that dark quiet night,
And showed us some of His glory!

The Greatest Book

There is a Book that's very old,
It's full of stories many have told.
God led men to write what was written,
Now He wants us to read and listen.

This Book tells us of God's big plan —
How He loves us and sent a Man,
Jesus Christ, God's Son, is His name;
He left heaven and to Earth He came!

He bled and died on the cross for us,
And we know He is the One to trust.
If we believe and trust in Him,
The Bible says we'll be saved from our sins!

Everything in the Book is true —
God would never, NEVER lie to you!
He tells how He wants us to live,
We need to love and always forgive.

We give thanks for this Book to read —
It has answers for all we need!
So, dear God, we'll try to obey
And read our Bibles every day.

The Holy Spirit

He was promised to us as believers
So many years ago.
When Jesus was ready to leave this Earth,
He told us so we would know.

The Comforter is one of His names
And He lives in us every day.
He guides us as we seek to know the truth
And He also can help when we pray.

One thing we must be careful of
And that is to not grieve Him,
So we must try to be sensitive
To the prompting we get from within.

There are times when He gives an idea
To do something kind for a friend,
And if we don't act on our impulse
The nudging may never come again.

So we need to pray to be ready,
To listen to the Spirit's voice,
For then our lives will be full and rich
And we'll really have cause to rejoice!

The Struggle

I am told in the Psalms to delight myself
In You, Lord, only You.
But there are so many distractions
In everything I do!

Oh, why is it so hard
To keep my mind controlled?
I've been trying ever since I was young
And now I'm getting old!

And still, Lord, there is struggle
To elevate each thought,
Just when I think there's progress
In applying all I've been taught.

I notice something not too nice
Is passing through my brain
And then I realize so well
From that I must refrain.

It's two steps forward, one step back —
It goes on every day!
Oh, Lord, I do so want to be
Consistent in every way!

Please help me, God, to rest in You
And delight in Your Holy Word.
I know that this is what to do
Though some think it's absurd.

The Scriptures are the helpful guide
For problems outside and within,
So if I absorb and apply Your Word
I know I'll commit less sin.

The Tongue

The tongue is an interesting muscle —
It never seems to tire!
It can be used to tell only the truth,
Or can prove that one is a liar.

It's used for very serious things,
Such as helping folks out of trouble;
Then other times it assists with fun
Like getting bubble gum to bubble!

We know that although it is not very big
This tongue is a powerful thing.
It can curse our Lord and our fellow man
Or be used when God's praises we sing!

James says in the Bible that it can direct us
Just like a big ship by its rudder;
But if we misuse it we soon will find
We're in trouble that may make us shudder!

If with pride we think we are pious
We probably need to get humble,
For unless we are able to bridle our tongue
It's easy to make others stumble.

The tongue will expose what is in our heart —
Of this we can be very sure.
Regular prayer and study of God's Word
Can help our thoughts be more pure.

No one but God can tame this beast —
Men have tried down through the years;
Yet still today this dangerous weapon
Can make others burst into tears.

But we should not be discouraged
In spite of this weakness we have;
For it is possible to say helpful things,
And words can heal like salve.

Do keep on praying and committing to God
The many words that you say;
And hopefully there will be some change
So you'll see progress, day by day.

The Trinity

Father, Son, and Holy Spirit,
All in one accord.
God, the Father, glorified
By Jesus Christ, the Lord.

Your Holy Spirit indwells us
When we believe in You —
So we are blessed by Your presence
In everything we do!

Though it's hard to understand
How You are three in one,
Yet we do believe it's true
And know You're surpassed by none!

Holy, Holy, Holy,
We lift our praise to You!
Help us as we focus
On You in all we do.

Thirty Pounds of Joy

She's loving and forgiving,
She always cleans her bowl.
She welcomes us with a wagging tail
And being petted is her goal!

Missy is the name we chose
For our darling beagle dog.
She's been with us for five years, now,
And she's a better pet than a frog!

There was one exciting evening though,
When her love of meat won out.
She grabbed and swallowed a sausage wrapper,
It went down without a doubt!

A trip to the vet was needed at once,
And the sausage soup was put on hold.
The company that came for supper laughed
When the sausage wrapper story was told!

So that time our doggie cost a lot —
It was $200 to pump her tummy!
But we still love her no matter what,
Even though she cost us all that money!

For every day she brings us joy,
Early in the morning — late at night.
She lets us know of her love for us
And makes us feel blessed and just right!

Thank You, God, for our Missy!

Trike Blessing

My eyelids are drooping,
My teeth aren't so white,
My skin doesn't fit —
But I can still ride my trike!

That's not all! I've had a fall
And can't do all I'd like.
But there's one thing I can do —
Yes, I can still ride my trike!

Trust

You, Lord, are the best One to trust;
You will never change at all.
And if I remember to lean on You
I'll be much less apt to fall.

So help me to do this each day of my life,
For then I'll get rid of worry.
Help me to pray through each problem that comes
Even if I'm in a hurry.

For You are there, just waiting to help,
I know this to be true.
So help me, dear Lord, as I walk each day,
For I know I can trust in You.

When Things Get Tough

When life gets tough
And things are rough,
Lord, lift our eyes to You.
Let us remember what You did on that cross
And all that You went through.

Help us to keep looking up
To gain the proper view —
And remember we don't deserve the pardon
We got from the sins we do (and did!)

For Jesus came, so pure and good,
He did everything the Father said He should.
And when He gave His life for me,
It was a wonderful gift to set me free!

So help me, Lord, to think on these things
When I'm in the midst of troubles life brings.
Give me a heart that loves You well
And an attitude to help my gloom dispel.

Thank You, Lord!

Wonderful Joy

Your Word tells me to be joyful
And sing praises to Your Holy Name.
For You are true and faithful
And You always remain the same.

So help me, Lord, each morning,
When I begin my day,
To lift my thoughts to You in praise
For guiding me along the way.

About the Author

Made in His image so many years ago;
Always protected — this I know!
Reared in a family with peace and love,
Joy with music — a gift from above.
Offspring I've had — two girls and two boys,
Reminders of lots of happy noise!
Illnesses big and small through the years —
Every time upheld by God through the tears.

Knee and hip replacements that were a success —
Awareness of God's gift of happiness.
Thankfulness in things both great and small,
His love and forgiveness over all.
Refreshment each day from a night of rest,
Yielding to God makes life the best.
Nostalgia sometimes as I get older.

Gratitude always seems to take over!
Reasons for joy overflow my cup —
Every time I remember that I should look up.
Eventually I will leave this ground floor,
King Jesus to praise forevermore!

Marjorie Greek celebrated her 90th birthday in 2022 in Oceanside, California, along with David, her husband of 68 years, her four children and spouses, many of her 13 grandchildren, and 13 of her 24 great-grandchildren. Besides writing poetry, she is passionate about music and enjoys singing in church choir with her husband. She plays piano for various senior sing-alongs and played violin in community and church orchestras for more than 70 years. Other hobbies include writing letters, visiting elderly, doing stitchery, and riding her senior trike. Her love of children is fulfilled when she spends time with any available grandchild or other youngsters in her church or neighborhood.

Made in the USA
Monee, IL
18 October 2024

68001827R00060